POND IMAGE

For
LAND-
SCAPE
Page 11

*Adolph
Dehn*

POND IMAGE

AND OTHER POEMS

By

JOHAN EGILSRUD

MINNEAPOLIS: THE LUND PRESS, INC.

1943

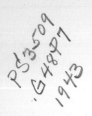

To Miss Amy Armstrong and Miss Elizabeth Atkins for their sympathetic help and encouragement; and to the artists Lucile Blanch, Adolf Dehn, and Wanda Gág for their gesture of friendship in making a gift of drawings for the poems.

Though the reflection in the pool
often swims before our eyes:
Know the image.

Only in the dual realm
do voices become
eternal and mild.

Ninth Sonnet to Orpheus
Rainer Maria Rilke.

CONTENTS

POND IMAGE

For THE FRAME   *Wanda Gág*

THE FRAME

Walking down a leaf-soft road
Through Autumn's splendid realm,
I saw, as in a far-off world,
Sharp, through the gold-frame of an elm,
The desolate, cold sea beyond.

And on the bleak horizon hung
Dead clouds of wintry white and grey
Beneath whose chill and heavy light,
Boats, ominous as birds of prey,
Moved darkly on.

And all of Autumn's secrets were
Deep in that vision, where the breath
Of life's most golden moment was
But as a frame to heighten death.

POND IMAGE

Flashes of joy,
Swift as the northern lights,
Shoot through my veins
As breathless I stand
In the darkness and stare
At the pond's bright
Image of you,
Fused with the pulsing flames
Of the night.

HOW CRUEL TO LOVE . . .

How cruel to love with an excess of power
And find in a hand's light pressure
A signal for ecstasy's joy-wild shower —
Yet to sense the return falling short of my measure;

To give in response to the lips' gentle brushing
A headlong kiss — but, after all,
To know that my heart's quick rushing,
As an answer, exceeds the call;

To lie long hours in trembling suspense
From meeting a faint caress,
And hear how the sleeper is lost to sense,
While I suffer my love's excess.

WHAT DO I WANT FROM BEAUTY?

Watching you, stranger, my heart
Beats a song of desire—
Not for you,
But for beauty that happens to linger
A moment around you.
I know nothing about you;
Yet, the curve of your neck,
The hair's black gleam,
The fall of your forehead,
The gentle yet strong
Bend of your nose,
The clear-cut planes
Of your mouth,
And the firm support of your chin—
These set my heart to beat
With excitement, desire . . .
What do I want from beauty?
Not you!

CIVILIZATION

When frustrate with the thought-confining permanence
Of stars and space, I turn to swiftly changing Time
To make my own change seem less quick, and thus defer
My certain doom; then, like a miser do I count
And measure yard by yard and pound by pound
And add and multiply by seconds everywhere;
I bolt the door and draw the heavy curtains close
To shut out Death's chill interstellar wind;
I light the fire and the shaded lamp
To find an ostrich-blind security within.

VARIATION ON AN ANCIENT THEME

Through the window's film of winter-grime
I see, behind a net of thin, charred twigs,
A heavy sky — dense with unspent rain.

Down at the garden's end, near a pale, smudged Pan,
The fragment of a broken fence hangs limp.
In the corner, an ornamental seat,
Yellowed, now, and smeared and lost,
(Its brave rococo swirls once moved
In time with summer's gayest moods)
Stands deep in dank and festering leaves.

Sad, sad and weary, is the time
With winter gone, and spring so far behind.

GREY DAY

Close clings the fog
To somber trees.
Sharp as a rasping knife,
A single bird-cry cuts
The muffled damp.
Choked by grey mist
Sits the rabbit, motionless.

From under the burden
Of a thousand miles of fog,
Man seeks in vain
The liberation of the skies.

PARK SCHWANENSEE

O world-unmindful, ivy-smelling spot
Of past and ghostly life —
In double absence of forgotten now, and then
What haunting loneliness of lonely sighs!
No pulse of life stirs ripples in the pond,
No breath of eagerness to lift dry leaves.
And mocking as the rouge on dead and withered cheek,
The frivolous pavilion's faded face
Lends to long forgotten love
Macaber life.

LANDSCAPE

The sheen of the lake is strangely white
Though clouds roll troubled and wild
Over black crags and rain-cut hills.
Like a dream-bound child,
It catches a fleeting mystic light —
From a world beyond thoughts and wills.

VISITANT

Into the all-prevailing green
Of haze around the trees,
The lawn, the misty sky,
The lake — pale green
At evening after wind —
The reeds along its edge,
The buds, not ripe nor red —
Into this vast and cooling green,
A foam-white horse
Carrying proudly a pale woman
Clad in red,
Moved slowly, and passed by.

SPRING QUESTION

Will the sweet freshness of these light-pierced leaves
And the peace-persuasive motion of the trees,
Will all the nesting softness of the clouds —
The cozy, buzzing home-sounds of the flies,
And these keen, joy-sharp calls
Of sun-inspired birds —
Will the faint messages of secret growth
And blossoming upon the air,
And the cool, healing presence of the lake —
Will all these animated messengers of peace
Restore this heart?

CELESTIAL FLEETS

The green-eyed lantern's tragic sheen
Makes sinister the close, black sea . . .
But far away —
With shocks of white, electric gleams
Through smudgy clouds,
The moon
Keeps vast celestial fleets
Of constellations in their course.

TO —

That in me which,
Facing this mist-shrouded scene,
Raises its voice in ecstasy,
Declaring its kinship
With beauty and truth —
That is also the source
Of my love for you.

LOVELIEST OF ALL YOUR KISSES

Loveliest of all your kisses
Are the kisses of despair
When your heart in haste dismisses
All restraint and morbid care,
And in glowing surge of feeling
Stamps the seal of life on me
With two joyous lips, revealing
That your soul at last is free.

ROMANTIC AGONY

The turbulent motion
Of the wind-torn tree
Is wild as the torment
Of passion in me.

The mad agitation
Of storm-clouds in flight
Has the terror and pain
I feel tonight.

And the death-like pallor
Of the moon on high
Is the pallor of my love
Fated to die.

DECAY

Why do the false-front buildings
On the dark hill-crest
Stare with such vacuous eyes
At the setting sun?
The gaping door-holes,
Toothless and sagging,
Add to their senile indifference.

Yet, the sun in the west
Is consuming heaven and earth
In a gigantic, cosmic furnace!
But the volcanic drama of fire,
The magnificent postlude of light
That ushers the earth
Into the darkness of space
Gets only a blank stare
From the toothless, old buildings
With their dirt-road in front,
And heavy, crowding hills around.

JOY REFLECTED

Moment! From the constant flux
Of time, be now detached,
A witness through these simple words
Of pure perfection, vivid and unmatched.

For in this instant, when I breathe
The spiced and snow-cooled mountain air
And hear the eager rustle of the leaves,
I sense a joy reflected everywhere.

It glitters in the trembling foliage,
And races through the bird's cadential song;
The light of heaven holds it in the blue,
And hills are urging it with rhythms strong.

A joy, so pure, so keen, must be
The pulse of life itself set free.

NORTHERN LIGHTS

The shimmering substance burns
Strange astral meanings in the skies.

Into my being's empty space
Blazes the luminous joy of your eyes.

RARE AND ADVENTUROUS MIND

Rare and adventurous mind!
By the force of your being
You draw from the commonplace
Luminous essence
And give to a dull-hearted world
Soul-quickening life.
When you walk through the woods,
Pushing eagerly forward,
You find
Where the waters run sweeter,
The trees stand fresher,
And horizons sweep vaster.
Or gathering flowers,
Always you look for the hidden petals,
Whose fragrance
Is haunting and rare.

But it is in your love
That the days are transformed
From tedious hours
To flaming eternity,
Burning away
The flesh and the earth
And the ticking of time
In a white focus of being
And joy.

THE CLOCK OF CTESIBIUS

Ingenious, and strangely wrought,
And full of rumours of a tragic fate,
The clock of old Ctesībius, the ancient Greek,
Lets fall warm tears from out a sculptured mask.
These gather in a cylinder, rise, and float
A manikin who, pointing to a nearby column's signs,
Catches the flux of time in seconds, minutes, hours.

So is it ever, then, in living terms
Of agony and joy, the record of man's fate.
So, in the empty timelessness of space
The center and the meaning is man's heart.

ESCAPE

Straight streets,
Stupid in regularity,
Dull, with the dullness
Of the too precise!
From your grey monotone I flee
To where the earthen path
Flows carelessly along
In gentle, changing gait,
Congenial to my thoughts.

To the soft yielding
Of the leisured slopes,
And to the urgent rise of hills
My soul responds as to the touch
Of loving hands . . .
Free from the clarity of rule and use
I shall escape, glad as a child
Just out of school,
To the sweet vagueness of the soul.

THE ARTIST

As swiftly you brush aside
The ferns to seek again
For flowers you hope they hide,
For beauty you hunt in vain,
Dew falls from the feathered leaves
In cold drops on your burning hand.
It is as if Nature grieves
With you for your fabled land.

SO LOVERS . . .

As trees
With load of leaf-weight
Drenched in rain
Stand not in bent and weary ways,
But stand in aromatic wealth
Of sap and scented moisture,
Feeling the burden of delight
In every rain-washed leaf —
So lovers,
Sensing the pain
Of over-rich, exalted joy,
Stand burdened, too — their hearts
Grown weighty with the tenderness,
The fresh, incessant stream of love —
And steeped in feelings, fragrant, full —
They yield — not from some heavy care
But from too great delight.

COMING FROM A HOUSE OF SORROW

Coming from a house of sorrow
I see and sense the spring —
But the winter of the heart I left
Blights every growing thing.

Abysmal as the pit of death,
Despair makes sinister the gay
Bright light, and turns to bitter taunts
The flaunting buds of May.

TO BETTY

I can speak of your face:
Your forehead is a temple-dome
Rising above a palaestra.
Your nose is an unachieved aspiration.
And the purposeful curve of your upper lip
Rules the playfulness of the lower.

I can speak of your body:
It is a struggle between action and thought
With beauty and force playing hide and seek.
But I can not speak of your eyes:
They contain universes.

THE KISS

Your secret kiss,
Suddenly given,
Tremulously firm,
Burned new
Miraculous meanings
Into my empty heart.

RESPONSE

With tongues that fit her every need
I answer Life: I give the plant
Sunshine and water. I give seed
And worms and twigs to nesting birds.
The playing cat, a mouse I grant;
The dog gets bones from me.

And to the heart that laughs and sings,
I bring the trumpets and the strings:
But to the soul that cries in pain
I open pity's reddest vein
And let love's blood flow free.

ANCESTORS

The brown eyes of my great-grandfather
And the blue eyes of my great-grandmother
Look in cool directness
From their periwig and pearls,
Questioning me what I have done
With their particle of life,
With my moment in the sun.

GHOST OF SUMMER

Poor, ash-grey moth
Whose fitful flutter
By my lamp
Brings from without
The ghost of summer
And the dust of death;
No blazoned butterfly
With summer's signs
Of sun and blossoming
Upon your wings —
Nor the rich season's bustling
And efficient bee —
Only a sad
And ineffectual ghost,
To flit,
And fall
Among dead flies.

HORRIBLY VOID OF EYES . . .

When drawn-up stiff and mummy-like in bed
I lie and watch my bony legs, and think:
Thus will I also look when I am dead,
When all that now is life in me will shrink
Till, like the juice that leaves the apple as it dries,
It leaves my body hard and withered where it lies.

Then, shuddering, I cover them with care
To keep the soul still warm within,
And on your name I call in my despair
To hold it as a shield against the grin
Of that white skull whose sockets I in terror see
Horribly void of eyes that now belong to me.

JUNE 1940

As the cries of the lost
Defenders of France
And the tragic blaze
Of bomb-racked London
Reach across the Atlantic,
As the grim glare
Of a burning civilization
Colors with blood
Every horizon—
I feel like one
Helpless on a crag
While wild waters whirl,
Sweeping away
His home,
His beloved,
His world!

Where can I find the stay
Of hope, faith, and charity?
Where the conviction that man
Still carries the sacred images
Of Greek temples
And Bach's holy masses?

But, when vainly I search
Among ruins and stars
Help for the dying
And balm for the scars,
Only Love, with its faith,
And Hope, Love's twin,
Point the way to a world
Of peace within.

SPRING DAY

Wind in the trees;
The blue day, sharp
With light, shot
From shattered waves;
High, swelling clouds
Blown seaward and west
Into the sky.
Once more the full lung,
The flush,
And the joy of the heart
Singing loud
Through the spacious halls
Of the day.

VENETIAN BAROQUE

Sin there is — and sudden death
In the blood-red reaches of that floor.
Decaying vice and dark intent
Crowd the brown shadows of that door.

The black, dead wind of destiny has slowly moved
The saffron curtain there between
The window arches, where they stand
Somber, opening on emptiness:

Above, a screen of writhing figures —
Images of men in agony —
Wild arms that rise deploringly
To pale and merciless Venetian skies.

For VENETIAN BAROQUE   *Lucile Blanch*

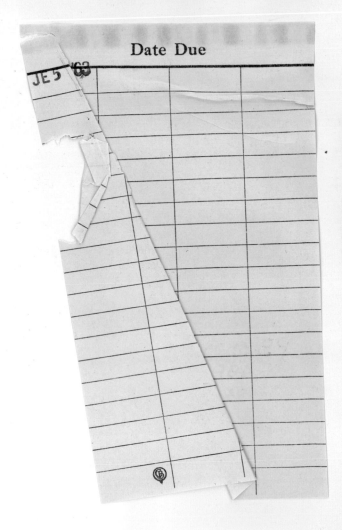

Date Due

JE5 '63